How To Hypnotize Anyone

Learn To Play Tricks Using Hypnosis Techniques

Table of content

Introduction 3

Chapter 1- What is Hypnosis? 4

Chapter 2- Does Hypnosis Really Work? 10

Chapter 3- Practice Hypnosis Using Powerful Scripts 12

Chapter 4- Basic Stage Hypnosis 15

Chapter 5- Using Hypnosis in Mind Encouragement 18

Chapter 6 – Experience Deep Trance for Yourself 22

Conclusion 24

PAGEREF _Toc428949170 \h 3

PAGEREF _Toc428949171 \h 4

PAGEREF _Toc428949175 \h 10

PAGEREF _Toc428949176 \h 12

PAGEREF _Toc428949177 \h 15

PAGEREF _Toc428949178 \h 18

PAGEREF _Toc428949179 \h 22

PAGEREF _Toc428949180 \h 24

Introduction

First I would like to thank and congratulate you on downloading "Hypnotize: 10 Ways to Play Tricks Using Hypnosis Techniques." You can certainly have some fun playing some harmless tricks on some friends or family members by learning how to hypnotize them. But make sure that they are well aware and in agreement to being hypnotized.

Scientists have studied hypnosis and have even managed to come up with their own techniques for heightening suggestibility, but even so there are still debates on how hypnosis occurs. You do not have to be a scientist to learn about or even become a hypnotist yourself. The best way that you can start to do this is by reading and learning the tricks gathered in this book that could help give you complete control over other people.

You must keep in mind that hypnosis can be dangerous so you shouldn't experiment on your family and loved ones once you become a hypnotist in a haphazard fashion. You can learn how to achieve success in life by tapping into the human subconscious!

Chapter 1- What is Hypnosis?

I am sure that you have heard of hypnosis before, when we hear the word hypnosis many of us picture some kind of brainwashing going on or mind-control. The truth is that in reality hypnosis is quite different from what we actually envision it to be. Hypnosis is basically a special psychological setting in which patients resemble a sleep-like state along with a functioning of awareness. A person that is in a hypnotic state tends to have a heightened focus on things and both intensity and concentration are present.

When people are under hypnosis they have a higher level of memory while at the same time they are able to tune or block out distractions. The term hypnosis actually came from the ancient Greeks; they were the first to use the word hypnos in order to denote sleep. In 1841 a Scottish surgeon (James Braid) used the term in order to describe nervous sleep. He practiced various hypnosis methods with Franz Mesmer. Finally modern hypnosis was introduced to the world. With modern hypnosis a person is induced into a relaxed state, then a number of suggestions and instructions are provided to them. These are delivered by the hypnotist, or it could also be self-administered. Today it is also used or practiced for therapeutic purposes known as hypnotherapy.

Hypnosis is also regarded as a subconscious trance which resembles sleep. Research has shown when persons are in a hypnotic state are aware of their surroundings and are in a focused attention which corresponds with a decrease in peripheral awareness. The subjects often show that they have increased control over suggestions while at the same time are in a sense of tranquility or peace.

The individual that is hypnotized tends to only take heed through the communication of the hypnotist and will respond in automatic fashion. The hypnotized person is able to feel, smell, and perceive things according to suggestions given by the hypnotist.

The earliest form of hypnosis is based on nervous or normal sleep. Before the real origin of the hypnotic state being based on abstraction and mental concentration. The abstraction of the mind had the ability or power to provide ideas, trains of thoughts and impressions. When a person is under hypnosis they can be guided in order to induce changes in perceptions, emotions, thoughts, sensations, experience, or behavior. The next hypnotic induction is based on the extended initial suggestion of the subject's imagination.

Induction and Trance

Hypnosis is preceded by an induction technique, traditionally this would be putting the subject into a hypnotic trance and is given a defining role or expectation. When the subject is in a trance state this denotes processes, levels of ecstasy and heightened state of mind, consciousness, and awareness. The term trance is associated with both meditation and hypnosis. Most people think of a trance as being in an altered state of consciousness. A trance is basically a dazed and half-conscious state similar to sleeping. People that are in this state are either unconscious, hypnotized or cataleptic state with complete absorption. When putting a person into a hypnotic trance, there are several induction techniques to choose from, of of these is Braid's eye fixation technique. This technique consists of looking into the eyes of the subject for a long time in order to apply the trance. Another technique uses theta meditation it is known as the induction of a trance state.

Subconscious and suggestion

The subject has to be in a subconscious state in order to achieve the effects of hypnosis. The subconscious state is when there is not a current focal awareness while subject is conscious. Some consider the subconscious as a type of replacement for the unconscious mind, yet there is still the presence of awareness. When a person is in a subconscious state of mind they are still composite to the conscious processes such as hearing, data collecting, and seeing. During this state the subject's conscious mind is not present so the mind tends to work instinctually. When the subject is in a subconscious state of mind they are more open to dominant ideas.

When an individual is in this state they are open to receive both verbal and non-verbal forms of suggestion, including self-hypnosis and a waking suggestion. Suggestions are used to activate a certain trail of thought within the subject. Most of the suggestions that are used in hypnosis come in a number of ideas, sensory perceptions such as hearing, smell, seeing and taste. When your subconscious mind is leading you tend to be more creative and you feel much more of a sense of freedom. Bodily sensations are provided by the subconscious mind, taste, touch, sight, and feelings. When a hypnotist affects the subjects subconscious they can trigger feelings in the subject of satisfaction, or mixed emotions and ecstasy. Our memories also find a home in our subconscious. When a subject is under hypnosis they are able to recall memories from their past that can help to resolve issues that they are having in their present life.

Contemporary hypnotism involves suggestions of direct verbal lines, indirect verbal suggestions, requests, insinuations, and rhetorical lines or figures of speech. A hypnotist may also apply physical manipulation, imagery, and tonality. Suggestions will differ according to what their delivery consists of. Most are given in an authoritarian setting, others are given permissively.

Post hypnotic suggestions are considered to bring about immediate responses while those that have been suggested during a subconscious state are designed to bring trigger responses which affects behavior. These effects can last for days or a lifetime. The effectiveness is based on achieving a certain specific goal.

Conscious and subconscious

Most suggestions are delivered to the subject during the conscious states while there are others that are required to be given in the subconscious state. Hypnotherapists practice this concept in order to change the unconscious processes which are embedded inside the mind. Some thoughts that are affected by the subconscious based suggestions are various fears, smoking, and stress. Suggestions that are targeting the conscious mind of the subject are based on the subject's attitude and things that they can control, such as their relationships with other people or the type of job they have. The nature of the mind can be changed with the right suggestions.

Chapter 2- Does Hypnosis Really Work?

Many of us when we think of hypnosis it is some kind of show that should be part of a carnival, or based on some cheap parlor tricks. Often hypnotics were portrayed as the villains or characters that would trick people into doing bad things. But beyond all the fakes and lies does hypnosis really truly work?

Hypnotherapy has been around as a long term treatment for both physical and psychiatric ailments. Most experts do believe that the trance state of human beings has the ability to heal various conditions. Let us consider the various factors that affect hypnosis' efficacy.

One of the factors that can effect hypnosis is susceptibility. Most people are open to change. They will allow suggestions into their life and they have control over their behavioral, physiological and subjective responses to hypnosis. It has been discovered through research that 80% of humans are moderately susceptible to change while 10% are low and 10% are high. Basically this study shows that people in general are susceptible to suggestion and pass hypnotizability. In the study it also revealed that people who suffer from dissociative identity disorder have the highest suggestive level followed by those with post-traumatic stress disorder.

The mental and physical state of a person is the next factor that affects the efficacy of hypnosis. Changing the mental state of a person is how hypnosis can be utilized. Through the use of proper hypnosis people that suffer from phobias, stress, identity disorder can overcome their conditions. Common health conditions such as cancer, the flu, and infections cannot be treated with hypnosis. The actual condition of the person does not effect the efficacy of the hypnosis suggestion. The efficacy effect will also depend on the type of hypnosis used.

Some types of hypnosis are more geared for the purpose of entertainment rather than assisting in clinical treatment such as the pendulum technique. When it comes to helping deal with stress and psychology forms such as the guided theta meditation often are used.

It is true that some people are more susceptible to hypnosis than others. A person's responsiveness to hypnosis does have a connection with their personality traits based on ability, imagery, gullibility, or submissiveness. People that are engrossed in other activities such as reading or listening to music have a higher chance of becoming hypnotized.

In some medical fields hypnosis has gained credibility and can be found in thousands of articles today. There is agreement that hypnosis can be utilized to help treat phobias, and chronic pain as well as other various conditions. We all have experienced one form or another of hypnosis. You may go into a trance like state while listening to a favorite bit of music.

Hypnosis does indeed exist and does have effects on people. You must keep in mind that a person that is hypnotized is neither asleep or awake. They are in a hyper-attentive state while under hypnosis which is responsive to subconscious directions. Just because a person is in a trance like state of subconscious this does not mean the person will become a robot. The person's current state of judgement and free will are still present while someone is in a trance. The suggestions the hypnotist will make to the subject will be based on the subject's current state.

Chapter 3- Practice Hypnosis Using Powerful Scripts

You must use powerful scripts in order for hypnosis to work. Using the right kind of script will largely determine the success of your hypnotic session. Some will use background music to help add to the effect of the script. Hypnotic scripts are based on what kind of effect you are looking to have. There are induction scripts that help the subject get into a relaxed state in mind and body. To deepen the trance there are deepening scripts. For therapeutic purposes there are therapeutic scripts, and then there are miscellaneous scripts that are used for various purposes.

For induction scripts some examples include hypno-prepation, body conditioning, confusional techniques, association, awareness technique, rapid method and stiff arm, deep relaxation. The analytic mind is improved using the confusional technique. To use this particular technique you must suggest to the client that they remember everything that has happened and that they store the information to their subconscious mind. You will then instruct your subject to forget everything in their conscious mind and listen closely to their subconscious mind.

With therapeutic scripts they are based on treatments. Some of these scripts may use healing before surgery, or slimming powers, permissive smoker script, anxiety and sleep easy script, guilt release script, confidence scripts, and arthritic script. When it comes to slimming scripts the subject is asked to picture how certain foods are affecting their body. You then suggest to the subject that they are slowly losing weight and as a result they are feeling better and healthier. There is is also therapeutic scripts known as the pain and confidence scripts. During the confidence script you will ask yourself to keep calm and relax. You will need to imagine that everyone that you communicate with is looking funny. In your mind you might picture them naked or with a funny costume on. After you have managed to focus your attention, you need to assure yourself that you are going to speak with confidence and eloquently. You will know that people that you interact with or communicate with respect you and you will lose your inferiority.

During the pain script ask your client to relax and enter into a dream. As your client descends into their dream, they are going to find themselves sinking deeper into a relaxing forest. Ask your subject or client to begin their descent then and count to 10. As you are counting to 10, ask your subject to go deeper and deeper. As they reach the lowest end of their journey, they will no longer feel pain, since they left it in the relaxing forest. Continue the count until the subject no longer feels pain.

Miscellaneous script is based on an assortment of effects. Using hypno preparation helps ensure that the trance is improved. To help a client forget a traumatic experience forgetting scripts are used. During a forgetting script you will encourage the subject to forget a traumatic experience by imagining it and re-experiencing it firsthand.

Try this sample script that will help you build confidence. Modify it depending on what kind of effect you are looking to achieve.

Begin using your favorite induction and deepener.

We have all experienced a special moment when we truly felt very proud of something that we said or did, or did not do. We may have received compliments from others that triggered a feeling of great pride within us.

Now allow your subconscious to provide you with a memory of a particular time in your life when you felt so good about yourself. It might be something that you accomplished, or something you worked hard at and got recognized for your efforts. The memory's contents don't really matter; what is important is the feeling that you felt at that special time in your life.

Expand on that memory once you have it, and visualize the situation you are in. Who is there with you? What are you doing? Where are you?

Now fill in the details of that special memory—what time of day was it? What time of year was it—was it snowing or raining or was it a sunny day? How were you feeling? Focus on the feelings.

Remember those positive feelings that you had inside. Were you feeling strong, self-assured, and confident? Take a deep long breath in through your nose, while you concentrate on making those good feelings stronger and more positive. At the same time you are taking in this breath press your right hand's thumb and middle finger together. In future anytime you take a deep breath in through your nose and press your right hand thumb and middle finger you are going to experience positive feelings. You can have these feelings anywhere you wish.

These feeling will become more and more a part of you making your feelings stronger and more positive.

Just remember when you want to feel confident and positive do that breathing and finger hold to bring forth those good feelings. You will feel those good strong feelings filling you up from head to toe. You are going to become a more confident and stronger person.

Chapter 4- Basic Stage Hypnosis

When just starting out as a beginner in hypnosis we will start with the basic stage-hypnosis. This is the simplest of the many tricks in the field of hypnotism. First find a group of people—close friends are ideal for this. Find the person in the group that is the most open.

Examine the group watching who is doing the most talking, try and distinguish the extroverts from the introverts within the group. Pick a favorite extrovert from the group. Strike up a conversation with the group in general, but start to direct your questions more to your target. It is difficult to choose a topic especially when you do not know your target. Make sure that the topic you choose is one that a person that is highly suggestible will notice. A great and simple topic to start with is the weather.

Start by telling the group that it is getting colder lately. But you should not just verbally express this you should start to rub your hands like it is getting cold, this is a form of non-verbal communication. You might even shake your body a bit too. After about several minutes when you see that your target is mentally receptive you should then ask "do you guys see something that looks like magic?" of course they will say yes. Ask your target for a bit of help. Let us presume that your chosen target is a man. Calmly ask him to stand beside you. Make sure that his feet are in a close position.

Now you begin to wave your hand in front of the group and slowly move yourself closer to the soon-to-be-hypnotized individual. When you are close enough, ask him to follow your hands with his eyes. While he is doing this move your hands to your own eyes. Even if he is already staring at you tell him to look directly into your gaze. Finally, you are now ready to make the simplest suggestion—tell him to sleep. You need to sound compelling and sure of what you are doing. The chances of your being successful in your mind-control also depend on a tug. The very moment you say to him "sleep" quickly pull his arm down—make sure it is strong enough to make him notice, but gentle enough to avoid causing him any pain.

The first few times that you may try to do this trick you may find that the person is not falling asleep. Your targets at best may just feel groggy. It does not mean that you have failed necessarily, it just means that some people are harder to hypnotize than others. Simply continue giving suggestions if the first one wasn't enough then try another (no more tugging). You must keep in mind that not all suggestions may work the way that you would like them to.

If you are giving commands that have negatives in them you may be sending the wrong message. Examples of negatives are "shouldn't, aren't, and isn't." The subconscious is not capable of processing these negatives. It is important that you give positive suggestions. You tell a person what to do instead of what not to do.

The next lesson in stage-hypnosis once you have managed to put someone to sleep, think of another command. Here is a tip: Make sure that you are always near the one that you have hypnotized to prevent sudden falls from occurring. You may want to tell your target to wake up, but inform them that they will only be able to say their mother's name, this is a good example of a follow-up suggestion. If you carried out this part of the trick correctly the person would follow what ever you said.

It is best to stay away from overly complicated commands, as well as those that could have a potential to be dangerous. The mind has its own self-defense mechanism. You need to make sure that you de-hypnotize anyone before you release them. It could cause problems for the person as they would be in a state where their mind is not fully alert. To get the person out of the trance you need to put them back to sleep. Once again count to three and command that they go back to sleep. When you want the individual to wake up you count to three and command them to wake up. Y

There is of course other ways to make this type of hypnosis more interesting especially if you have an audience to amuse. Instead of just having the person wake up you will make some relaxing suggestions such as:

- you will have more energy when you wake up for the rest of the day

- you will feel so happy when you wake up

These are just two great examples of what you can do when you have managed to successfully hypnotize someone. Keep practicing with this basic form of hypnosis technique before you move forward into learning more complicated techniques. Try and practice with different groups of people. You must keep on doing this basic technique until you have perfected it if you truly want to be a hypnotist. Once you have managed to master stage-hypnosis you are then ready to move on to other hypnosis techniques.

Chapter 5- Using Hypnosis in Mind Encouragement

Using hypnosis to help solve fear and disappointment in a person's life is a way that you can help people to deal with these strong negative emotions. You can make them much less harmful than they are normally through the use of hypnotic techniques. You may know someone that is fighting these dreaded feelings, using the proper hypnosis you could help them to battle these by offering the right kind of help to them.

Using hypnosis to fight against fear and disappointment is not that difficult. The first step in doing this is to find a place that is going to be comfortable for the person you are going to hypnotize and yourself. You want it to be a place of calm and peace that has a relaxing feel to it.

You will sit yourself beside the person offering them to either lie down or sit up what ever position they feel most comfortable. Tell the person that they are going to be in a daydream kind of state that they are not going to be asleep. Due to the mind's self-defense hypnotism is virtually harmless. Many people view hypnosis as what they see in movies where a person is hypnotized and turned into a slave or taken advantage of while under hypnosis.

You may want to dim the lights in the room and ask the person to close their eyes, while you are having your hypnosis session. Make sure that there is no gadgets in the room that make sounds this will only distract the person that you are trying to hypnotize. Once you have everything and everyone in their places and sorted you are ready to begin the hypnosis session.

In a cool calm voice tell the person that they will be able to recall everything. This is a way that you will ensure the person that they will not forget the hypnosis session after it has ended. You can help guide them by asking them to think of the perfect relaxing setting. Once you have gotten the person to mentally imagine that they are off at a relaxing vacation spot then you move to the body-part relaxation.

At this point you want to help the person to relax their body thoroughly. Tell them things along the lines of "your arms are no longer tense, but are totally relaxed, they are becoming more relaxed with each passing moment. Use this approach with other body parts such as legs and hips. The more descriptive you are the better the results will be.

Make sure that each body part is fully relaxed before you move on to the next one. Once you have completed this part you will then shift back to relaxing in a general sense.

Tell the person that they are feeling a degree of peace and calmness that they have never felt before, when the person hears your voice the feeling of tranquility will become even greater. Keep repeating this suggestions several times before trying another message.

Now start to lead the person's imagination towards feelings of courage and hope having positive thoughts and feelings. Tell them that when they listen to your voice their confidence is going to grow and that they are go to feel less disappointment with themselves.

Tell them they are going to evolve into a person that is confident. You need to come up with more mentally-stimulating lines. Here are some good ones you may want to try:

- imagine yourself conquering the greatest obstacles in your life

- feel how easy it is to become successful

- disappointment is oozing out of your body, you are being cleansed of disappointment

- feel warmth, hope and healing in your heart

It is important to match the suggestions with the issues that the person is having. You also must keep in mind that saying things once is never enough. You must use repetition, this is one of the main keys to success in hypnosis. You need to always repeat your hypnotic suggestions at least several times.

Also make sure that you keep your tone of voice steady and consistent. Even when you are trying to pull someone away from dark depressing feelings you need to keep your tone of voice steady and calm, do not sound like a cheering section. Loud sounds will break the trans so you must keep everything during the session calm and peaceful as well as quiet. Even when you are giving very encouraging suggestions say them slowly, calmly, and softly.

Once you have given all the suggestions that you were able to come up with it is time to slowly end the session. You may want to use the count to three trick. You may find that the person has been lifted and appears to have gotten rid of the negative emotions, don't assume that you are now able to take on serious cases of people suffering from severe depression or emotional disorders.

Those that suffer with more severe emotional conditions will have more rigorous therapies prescribed to them. Only the medical hypnotism experts are skilled to tackle the greatest concerns such as trauma, physical pain, and severe depression. If someone you know is asking you for help in these areas you should guide them towards a credible hypnotherapy specialist.

If you want to become a better hypnotist it is not about making people do all kinds of crazy things. You can use hypnosis to benefit people in making them feel better. One way of accomplishing this is to put the mind and body in a relaxed state. Using this technique of hypnosis you can help people to get rid of stress at a subconscious level. Using the relaxation method you can help people to feel much happier instead of feeling stressed out.

You use the same technique that was mentioned in the previous chapter. Using the relaxation technique by finding a quiet place where you and the person that you are hypnotizing feels comfortable. You will go through the whole process of getting the person to the point where they are feeling both relaxed in mind and body.

Make sure the person has their eyes closed and the room is dimly lit, and has no other distractions in it. When you are sure the person is in a total state of relaxation you guide them by expressing to them that they need to place themselves in a stress free environment a place that they can picture in their minds as somewhere they would feel totally relaxed.

You are using basically the same relaxation technique you used for fighting against fear and disappointment. But here you are going to suggest ways for the person to release the stress that is built up inside them and replace it with a feeling of total calm and peace. Tell them that when they wake up they will no longer feel the stresses they have been burdened with, but instead will feel totally relaxed and calm.

Chapter 6 – Experience Deep Trance for Yourself

In this final chapter we will look at how hypnosis and meditation are similar, both of these methods are used to access deep thought. Hypnosis is based on trance that involves a number of suggestions that are given by the hypnotist to the subject, of which could make dramatic changes in the subject's life. We can use meditation to access deep thought using relaxing sounds and brain wave frequencies. Both of these have effect during deep trance and both are capable of changing our way of thinking.

Guided theta meditation if one of the main practices in meditation. In this form of meditation theta waves are featured which have a guided effect on your way of thinking. It provides powerful combinations of delta and gamma waves in order to help increase your clarity and flow of thinking while at the same time washes away your built up stress.

There has been many people that have used this form of meditation and have stated that it has helped relieve them of headaches. You can achieve Theta waves through the use of advanced meditation. It is considered to be the most elusive and powerful state that you can experience with your brain. It also provides you with a way to tap into the deeper levels of Theta.

Using this form of meditation will also show you how to tap into the large burst of electrical power that is referred to as kindling, which will ignite your insight and inspiration.

Once your Theta waves increase in strength, your brain activity will also be lowered, making you much more intuitive and it will also help you in reaching your creative depths in your brain.

When you are in a meditative state you can then apply self-hypnosis in order for you to change the way that you think. You can use the scripts mentioned in the previous chapter in order to change the things that you do not like about your life. You can use the confidence scripts to help boost your confidence when dealing with other people in personal and work situations.

Learn to utilize the pain scripts to help rid yourself of the aches and pains that you suffer from with your body. You may also use Theta to help heal others that may be suffering. Tap into the hidden parts of your brain with Theta meditation, gaining a full understanding of your brain and its awakening power.

Using guided Theta meditation you can enter a hypnotic state on your own and cause positive, change in your life through this method. Theta meditation is a common form of meditation that monks have practiced for many years, but with technology today we can enter Theta meditation with a guided audio.

Conclusion

Thanks for downloading my book, I hope you were able to find the information about hypnosis that you were looking for. The next thing for you to do after this is try applying what you have learned from this book!

Finally I would like to ask you to leave a short review on Amazon if you enjoyed my book. I would greatly appreciate it, thanks again and good luck with the hypnosis!

Printed in the USA
CPSIA information can be obtained
at www.ICGtesting.com
LVHW011156051023
R17915800009B/R179158PG759921LVX00021B/15